THE POOPY HIGHWAY

An Imperforate Anus (IA) & Anorectal Malformation (ARM) Story

Written & Illustrated by
Andrew Deutsch & Rori DuBoff

ISBN: 9798320145587
Library of Congress Control Number: 2024906102

To our wonderful son, who gives us so much joy, love and inspiration (and great ideas for this book!).

To the many family, friends and healthcare professionals who've helped guide and support our family on this journey, including:

* Dr. Wood & the CCPR team at Nationwide Children's Hospital, Columbus, OH
* Ronald McDonald House, Columbus, OH
* Dr. Levitt, Children's National Hospital, Washington, DC
* P. Stephen Oh, M.D., Weil Cornell, New York, NY
* Dr. Janet Woodward, Willows Pediatric, Westport, CT

And to all the other families on similar journeys. 

One day after school, Ian was at the playground with his friend Lily.

Ian was having so much fun going down the slide, while Lily was climbing across the monkey bars.

They were so happy to be playing.

Ian was having so much fun playing with Lily that he didn't want to stop. But Ian needed to tell his daddy something.

Ian ran over to his daddy and said, "I have to go to the bathroom. I think I've had an accident."

Ian's daddy said, "That's ok. Let's get you cleaned up and head home. It's almost time for dinner."

Ian waved goodbye to Lily and headed home with his daddy.

After eating dinner and going to the bathroom, Ian thought about the accident at the playground, and the time he spent on the toilet every day.

So, during storytime that night, Ian asked, "Mommy? Why do I have accidents and spend so much time on the toilet?"

His mommy said, "That's a great question.
Let me read you a story about when you
were born and your poopy highway."

Once upon a time, a beautiful baby named Ian was born to the luckiest and happiest parents in the world.

Ian's little body was a magical maze
inside, full of twists and turns.

His heart, brain, and lungs all worked
beautifully.

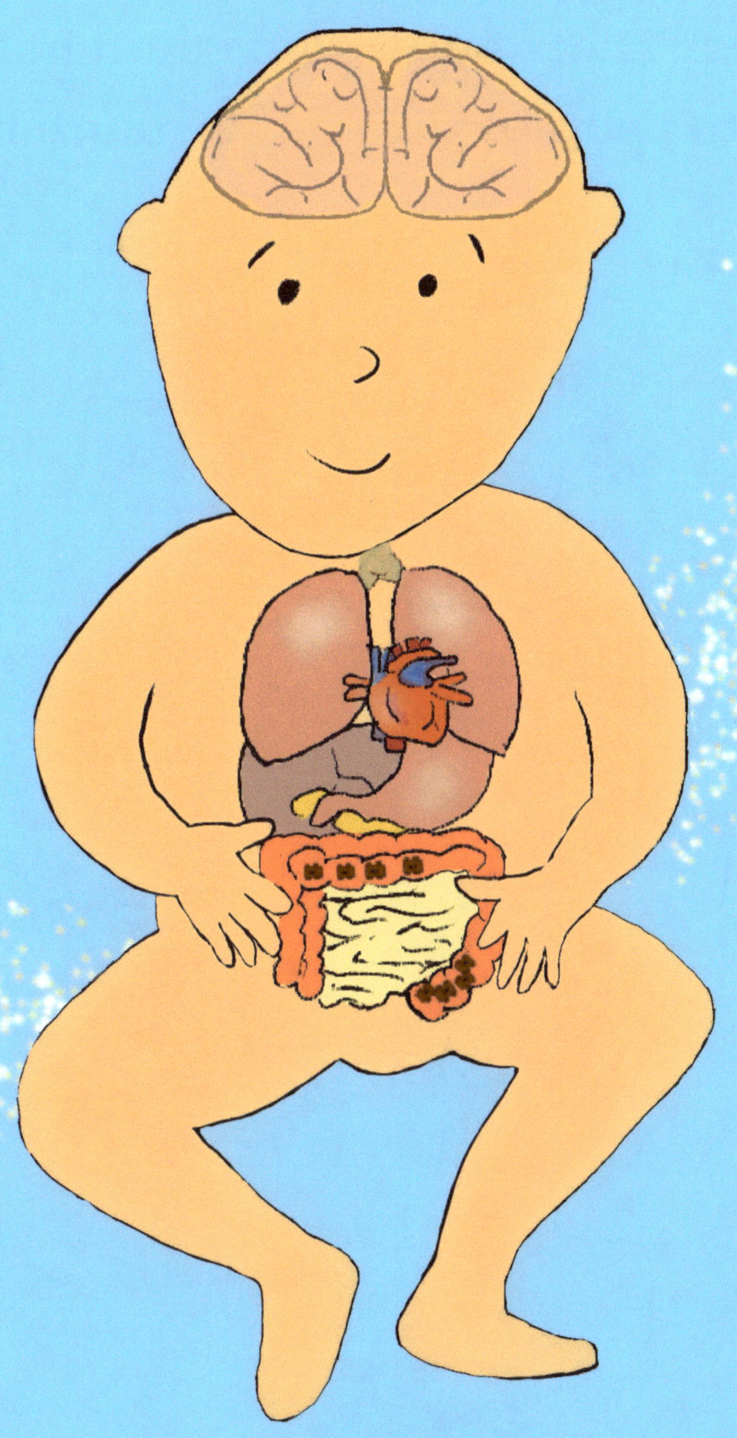

Yet there was a problem...
Every baby is born with a colon, a long
tube near their belly. The colon helps turn
food into poop that exits through the butt.

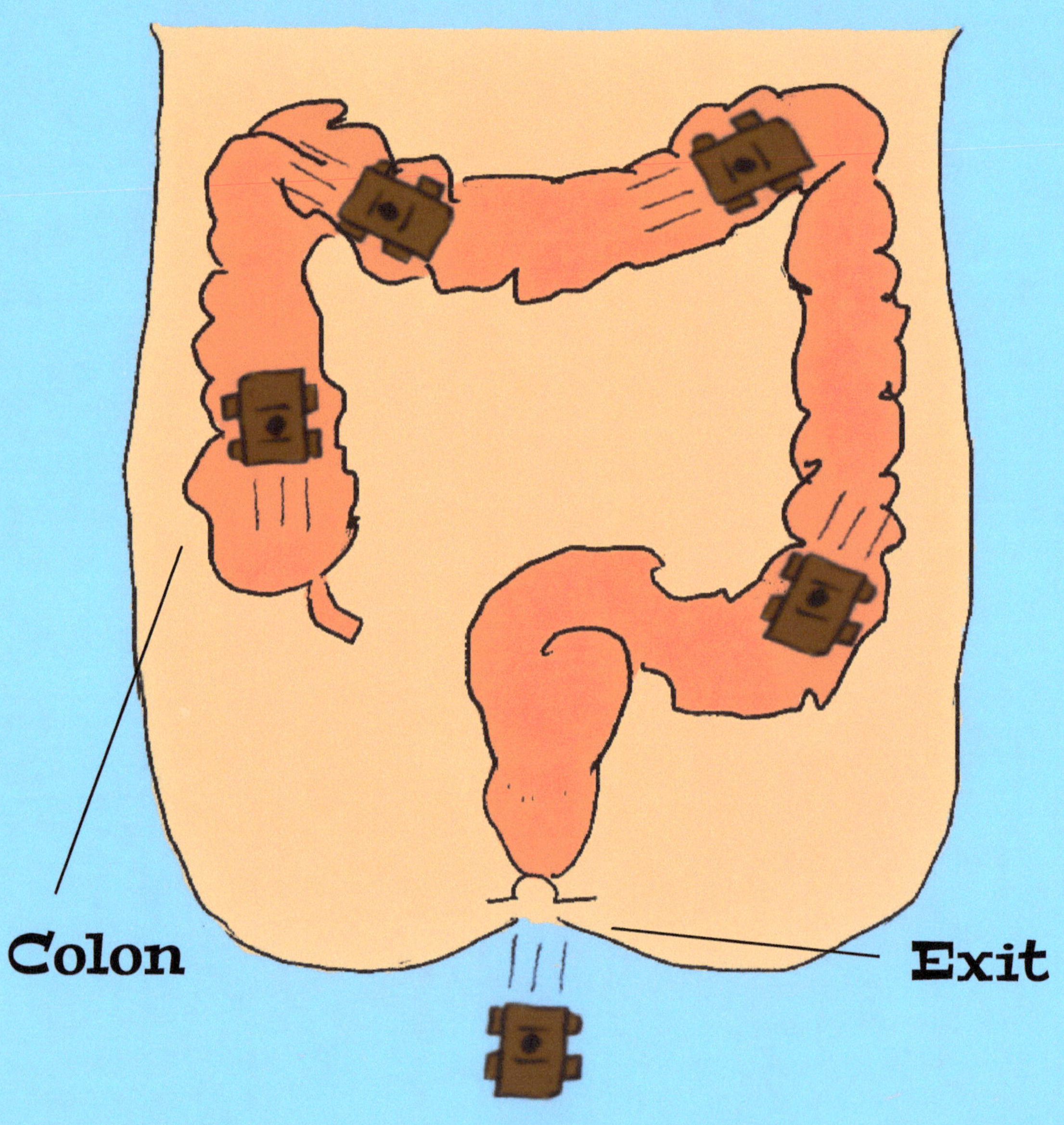

Ian's poopy was stuck in his colon because
he had no exit through his butt.

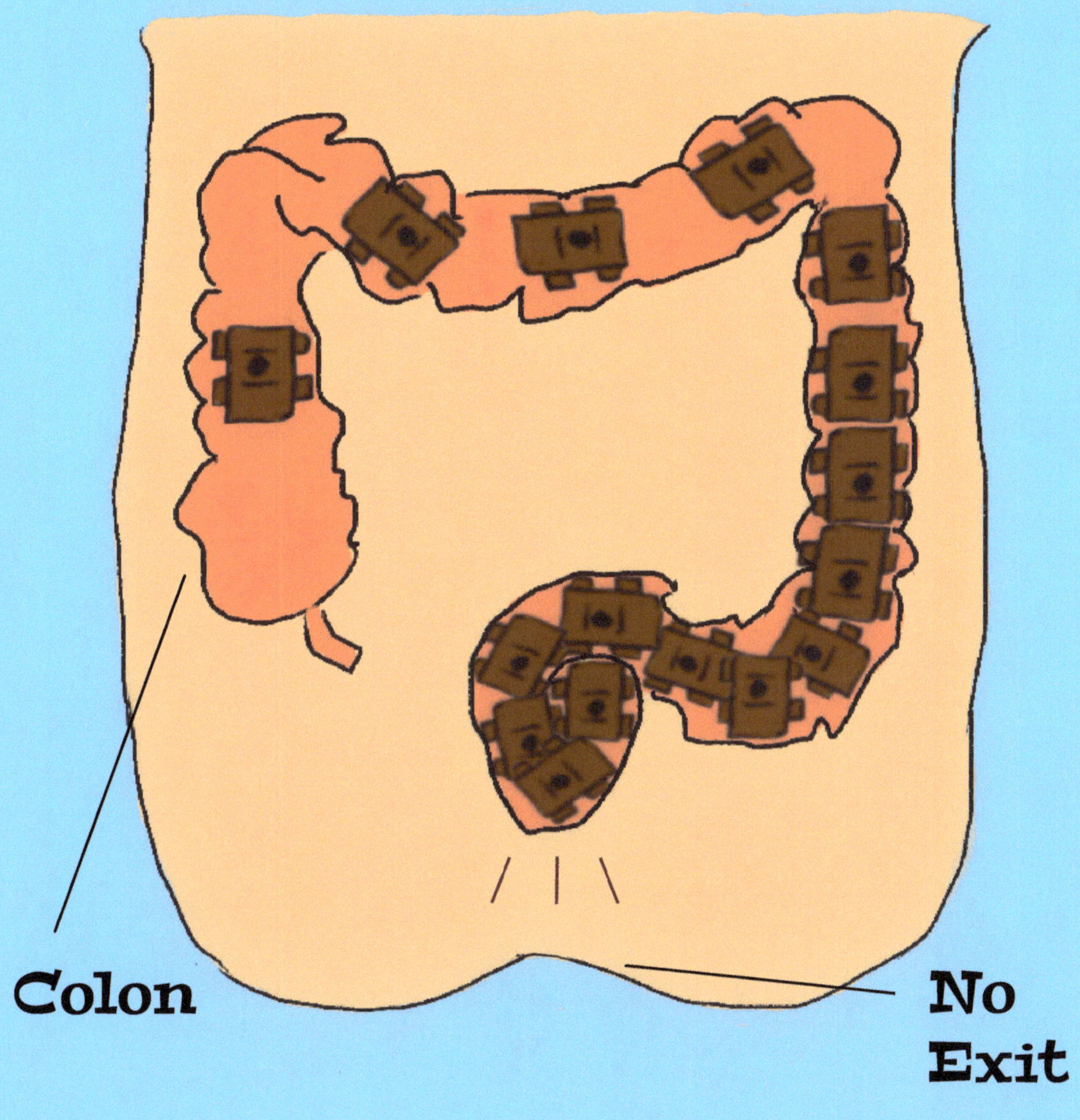

Ian's mommy continued, "We call the
colon the "poopy highway" because it is
like a long road that poop travels to exit
the body.

Now, imagine that without an exit,
no poopy could move forward or leave the
poopy highway. The poopy are now stuck in
a traffic jam that makes them unhappy!"

LET US OUT!
NO WAY!
GRR!
BOO!

Because of the poopy traffic jam, the doctor came to see Ian's parents at the hospital right after he was born.

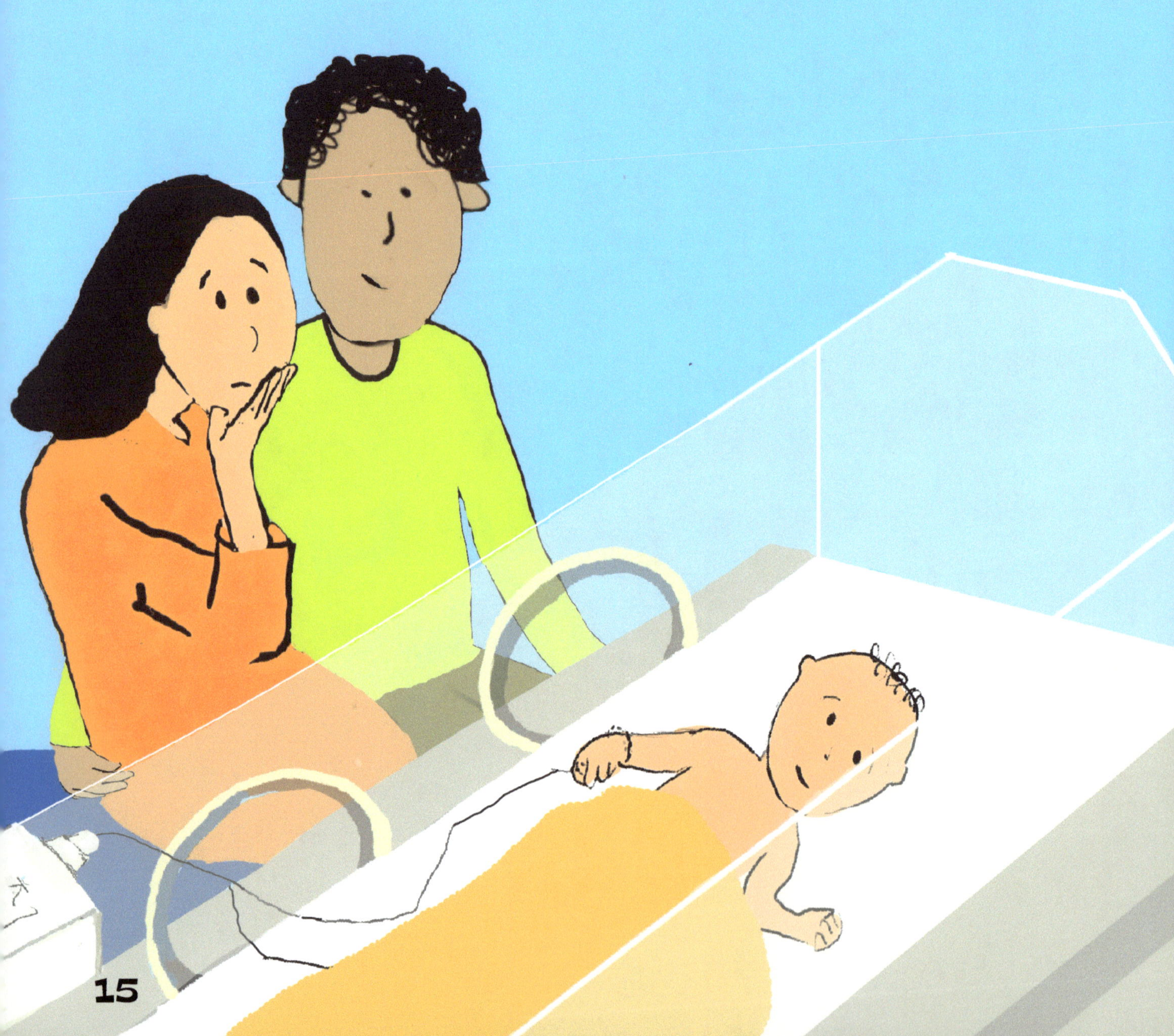

The doctor explained, "Ian has a health condition called imperforate anus (IA), also known as anorectal malformation (ARM). This means poop cannot leave his body unless we create an exit."

To help the poopy come out, the doctor
performed surgery on Ian. Now, the poopy
could exit through a temporary opening in
Ian's belly.

The poopy was happy it could now travel
outside of Ian's body into a tummy pouch.

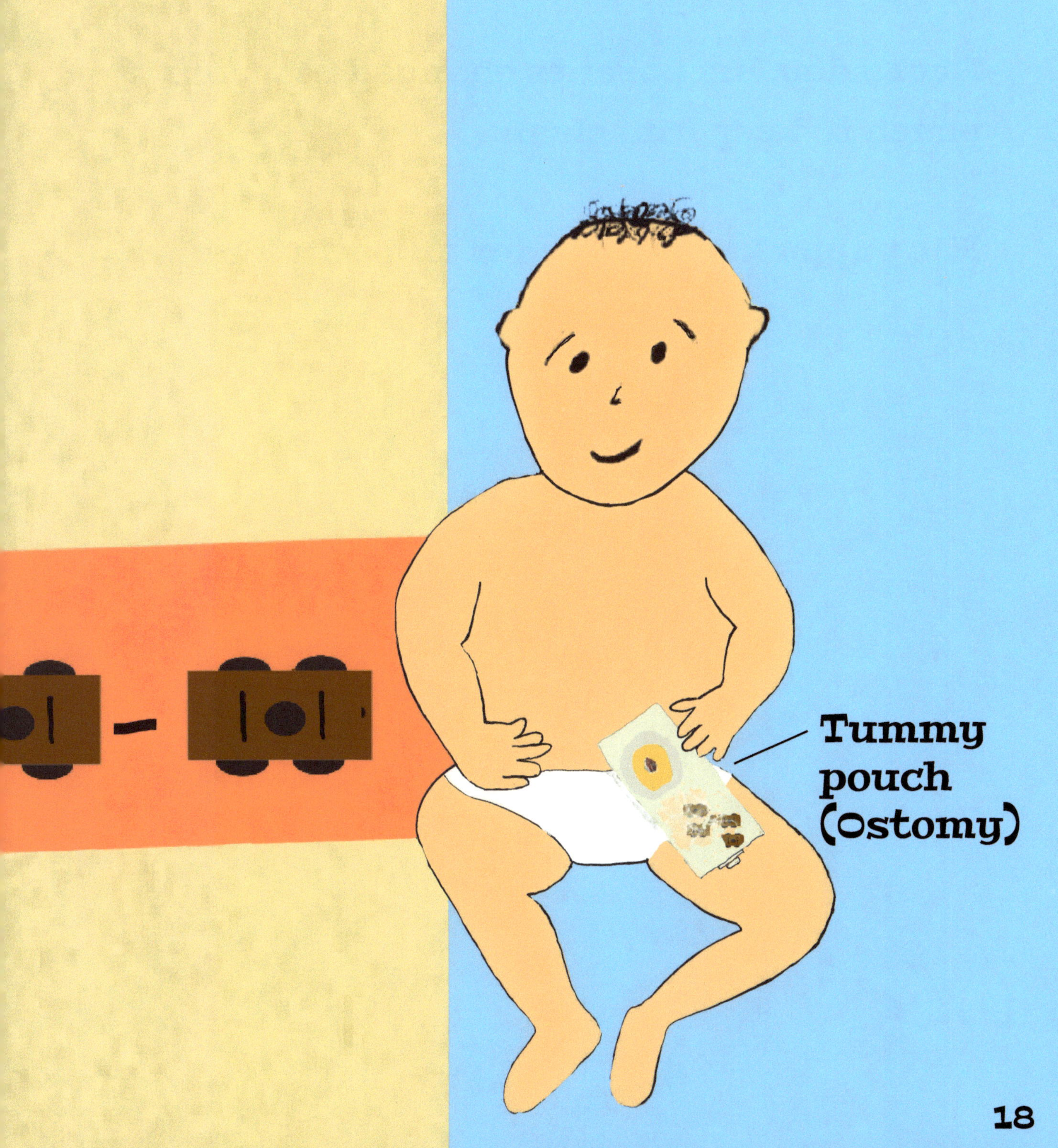

Tummy pouch (Ostomy)

Ian spent his first 6 months with a tummy pouch.

Every day, his parents changed his tummy pouch to keep him clean.

His puppy kept watch for any accidents.

When Ian was bigger and a few months older, the doctors closed the belly opening.

A small rainbow-shaped mark was left on Ian's belly.

The doctors then performed a second surgery that made an exit through Ian's butt, like most other kids have.

Over the next year, just like other kids,
Ian pooped in a diaper.

And pooped.

And pooped, just like other kids.

Ian's poopy enjoyed taking the new
bottom exit.

This made the poopy, Ian and his parents
very, very happy.

WHEE!
LET'S GO!

And then, when Ian was a 3-year-old, he started to poop on the potty!

But Ian still needed help to keep the poopy traffic moving every day.

To help make Ian poop, his parents gave him mighty chocolates and big bang drinks.

Even though the puppy wanted some chocolate, they didn't get any. Not even a taste!

LAX

Still, there were times when the poopy got stuck in traffic jams and Ian's belly hurt.

Ian didn't always know when his poopy traffic was stopping or going because his body couldn't always feel it.

Accidents started to happen, which Ian did not like.

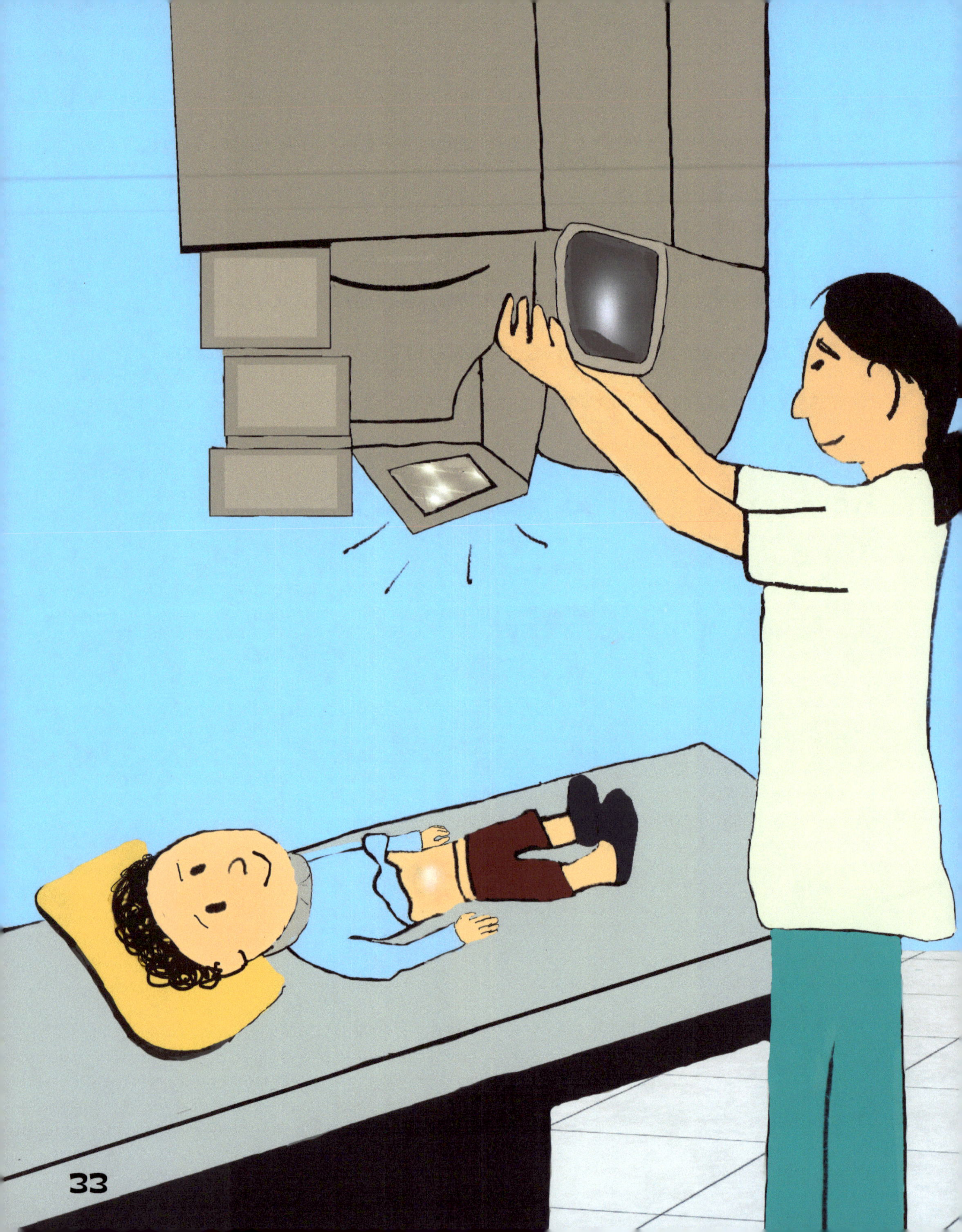

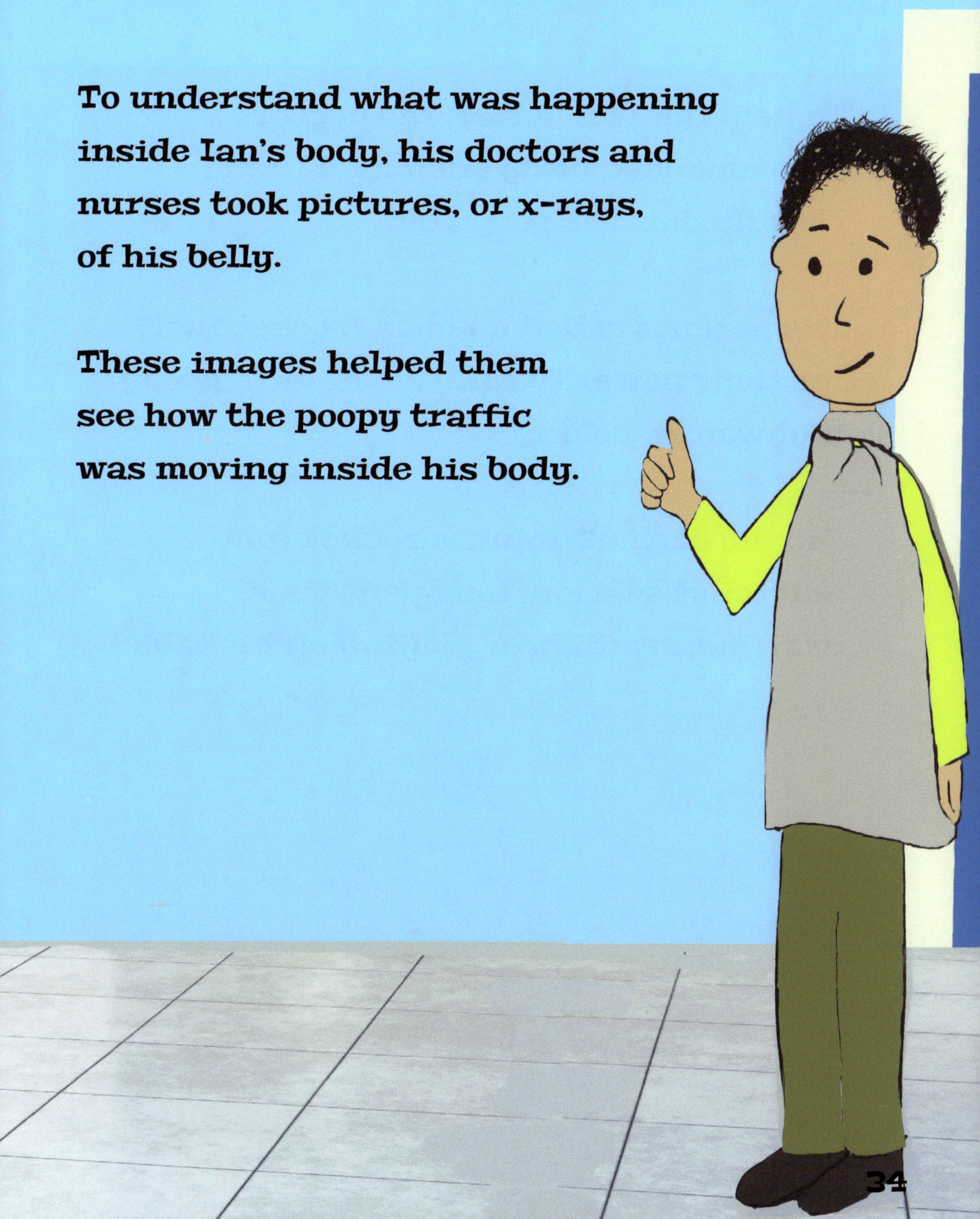

To understand what was happening
inside Ian's body, his doctors and
nurses took pictures, or x-rays,
of his belly.

These images helped them
see how the poopy traffic
was moving inside his body.

To help Ian feel better, his doctors
recommended daily enemas, a liquid
that flushes the poopy out.

His parents called enemas "rocket fuel"
for their power to fully clean Ian's poopy
highway, or colon.

During each 45-minute rocket fuel
and toilet session, Ian spent time
drawing, reading, or playing on his tablet.

Ian also started understanding which foods could help him keep the traffic flow steady.

Ian learned that doing exercises could give his belly superpowers to help control the traffic on the poopy highway better.

His mom smiled. "Ian, do you have any
questions about your story?"

Ian nodded. "Am I the only one who needs
rocket fuel? What about other kids?"

"You're definitely not alone," his mom
reassured him. "Lots of kids and adults
take special steps to keep their poopy
highways running smoothly.

Every kid has their own unique body
to take care of. Everyone has their own
unique way of making their body work
the best it can."

Ian's mommy continued, "While some kids, just like you, use rocket fuel, many stay clean by eating high-fiber foods.

Many people also get help to go to the bathroom by taking laxatives."

"Exercise is also a big help in keeping the muscles near your poopy highway strong."

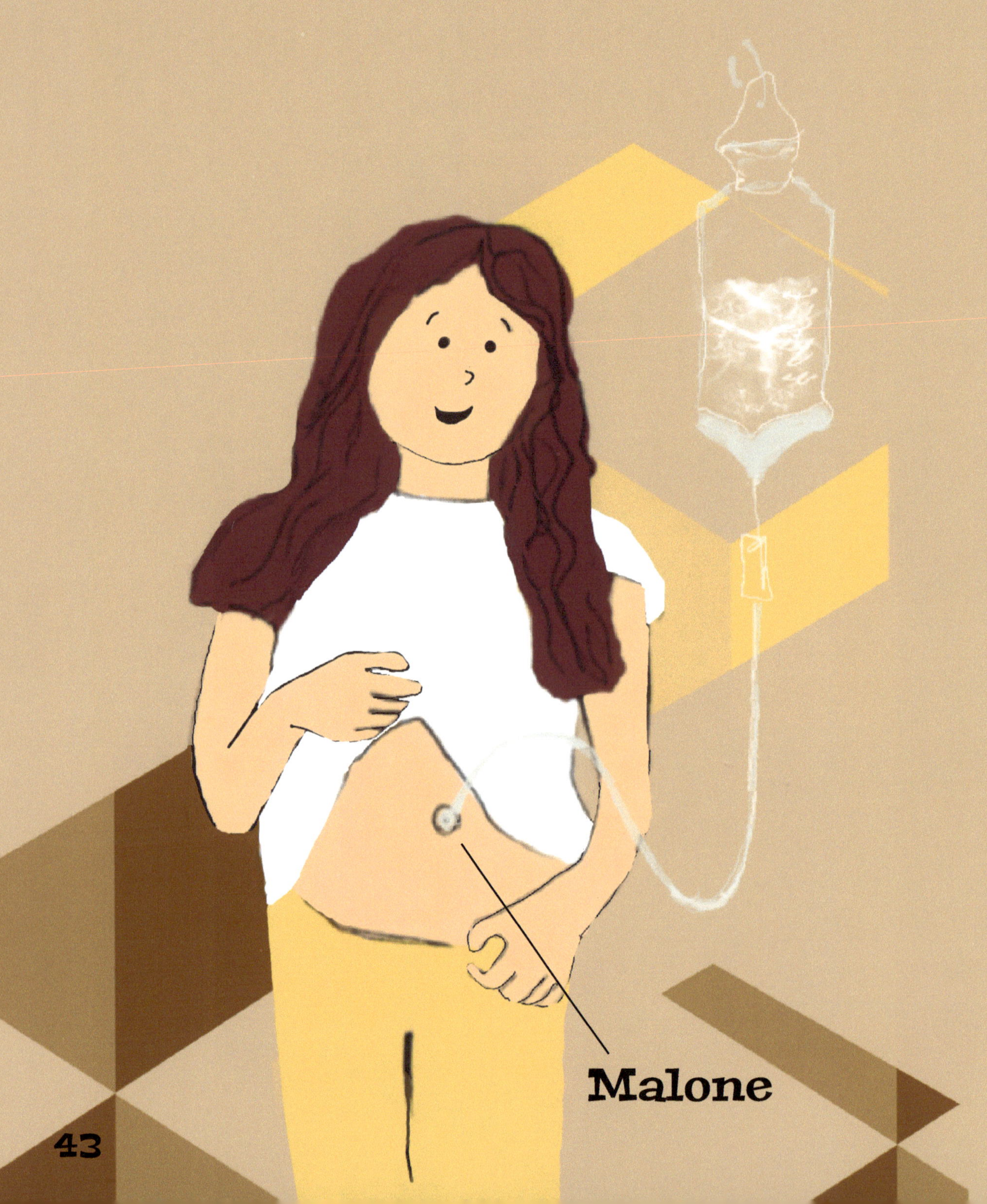
Malone

Ian's mommy continued, "There is another way kids and adults with IA/ARM can take care of their poopy highways, called a Malone.

A Malone is a surgery which lets kids and adults put rocket fuel through the belly button at the top of the poopy highway, instead of through the bottom.

A Malone can make it easier for people like you to clean their poopy highway all by themselves!"

"Remember," Ian's mom said, "we will ask more questions next time we see your team of doctors and nurses."

"The team loves seeing you get better and better at keeping your poopy highway moving!"

So, as Ian grew up, he became more confident about the different ways he could manage his poopy highway.

Ian knew he could do anything he wanted, just like his friends.

And with lots of love from his family
and friends, Ian grew up happy and strong.

Some Helpful Information

Glossary

- **IA (Imperforate Anus):** Also known as anorectal malformation, is a birth defect where the opening of the bottom is too small, in the wrong place, or missing altogether. This makes it hard for babies to have normal poops. It affects about 1 out of every 5,000.

- **Poopy Highway:** A long windy road inside the body called the colon. It's where poop travels before it leaves the body.

- **Exit:** The anus, a hole in the bottom where poop leaves the body.

- **Surgery Plan & Repair:** IA surgery required which often includes 1) Colostomy 2) Primary Anorectoplasty (PSARP) 3) Closure of colostomy followed by 4) bowel management and potentially, 5) Malone.

- **Belly Pouch (Ostomy Bag):** A small bag that sticks to the belly. It collects poop from a tiny hole in the belly, called a stoma. This helps people who can't go to the bathroom in the regular way.

- **Mighty Chocolates and Big bang drinks:** Edible and drinkable forms of laxatives that help people poop better to avoid constipation. Medicines include ex-lax and Miralax.

- **Rocket Fuel:** Also known as an enema, it is a saline water-based solution (often mixed with glycerin and other stimulants) that helps clean out the poop in the bottom. It is put into the bottom with a tube. Sometimes, a special surgery called a Malone procedure lets doctors put the rocket fuel into the belly instead.

- **Malone:** An appendicostomy or MACE (Malone antegrade colonic enema), is a surgically created channel between the belly (abdomen) and the colon. This lets a flush, or enema, be given at the beginning of the colon instead of at the end through the rectum.

Suggested resources

- Nationwide Children's Hospital: www.nationwidechildrens.org/lp/ccpr/imperforate-anus
- Boston Children's Hospital: www.childrenshospital.org/conditions/anorectal-malformation
- Colorado Children's Hospital: www.childrenscolorado.org
- Cincinnati Children's Hospital: www.cincinnatichildrens.org/service/c/colorectal
- Children's National Hospital: www.childrensnational.org/get-care/departments/colorectal
- Facebook Groups: Imperforate Anus USA Support Group, Colorectal Support Network, Center for Colorectal and Pelvic Reconstruction at NCH, ONE in 5000 Information Group